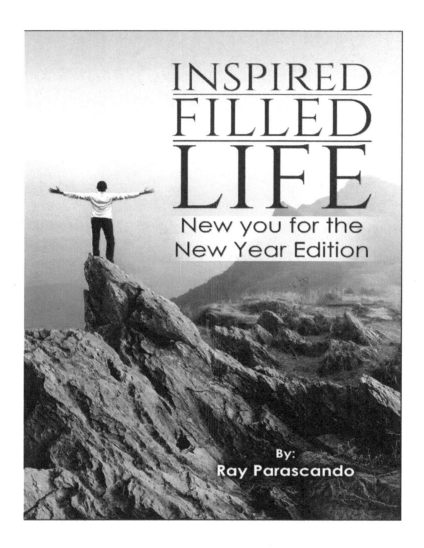

The Inspired Filled Life, New You For A New Year Edition

Written by Ray Parascando, 2022

Table Of Contents

Dedication

Drama can sometimes drain every ounce of patience and strength you have left. Even on a relatively normal day, discouragement can be in the forecast. That is why this book is dedicated to you!

Your life matters to God and others! So, you need and deserve inspiration from God, which is what this book will deliver. Here you will find encouragement from the Scriptures that will inspire you to know that you are God's masterpiece and He has plans for you.

"For we are God's masterpiece. He has created us a new in Christ Jesus, so we can do the good things he planned for us long ago." -- Ephesians 2:10 (NLT)

Before you start, let me thank you for taking the time to read this book. I realize there are many choices, and your time is valuable. Thus, I pray that God uses this material to impact you in incredible ways.

I also want to thank my family, friends, and Crossroads Church for supporting me in this endeavor. May God bless you as you think through these Scriptures and words.

Your Road Map

You are reading or listening to a road map, not just a book! As you begin a new day, month, or year, consider this book as a map that will help guide you to new heights in your relationship with God. You will also find directions to help you navigate old pesky problems that act as obstacles. By God's grace and your investment of time, you will discover a *"new you"* in this new year.

To maximize the Inspired Filled Life, New You For The New Year, take one day at a time and complete the Thinking About My Inspiration section.

May God bless and inspire you!

Your Next 31 Days

Did you know that seven months out of the year have 31 days? *(January, March, May, July, August, October, and December)*. Given that, don't you think it's wise to have a game plan to take at least one of these months to reset your focus on God and finally break through some of your barriers? Maybe one of your barriers is fear, weight, faith, pride, or adversity. Thankfully, the Bible tells us to be good managers of our time so that we can realize change. Psalm 90:12 says, *"Teach us to number our days, that we may gain a heart of wisdom."*

Perhaps you'll agree that we are drowning in information and starving for transformation today! Your next 31 days of going through Inspired Filled Life, New You For The New Year, regardless of where you jump in on the calendar, will challenge you to think through God's promises, plans, and purpose.

Making the LEAP!

I pray that you experience exponential growth relationally, emotionally, mentally, and spiritually as you go through this book. To ensure these goals, we have placed some tangible and interactive steps at the end of each chapter titled: *"Thinking About My Inspiration."*

Here are the action steps to take:

Reflective thinking: At the end of each chapter, there will be a summary statement that you can reflect on throughout the day.

Review verse: Each chapter will feature a key verse from the Bible that reinforces the day's lesson.

Responsive prayer: After finishing the chapter, there will be a prayer based on the devotional for the day.

These steps will help fortify all that you are absorbing from the devotional.

Fresh Start With God | Day 1

"Every moment is a fresh beginning." — T.S. Eliot, Author

"Behold, I am making all things new." — Revelation 21:5 / ESV

You need a fresh start!

Whether you have it all together or you're a mess, life is a mind game that takes a toll on you. More than likely, you have taken creative approaches to address the reality of being drained or dissatisfied. Typically a change in the calendar, scenery, occupation, or relationship offers a sense of optimism, but in the big picture, it isn't enough. For those opportunities and others like them to be meaningful and successful, you first need a fresh start with God!

There's an old saying, *"A rising tide raises all boats."* See, a fresh start with God lifts all the ships (responsibilities, resolutions, and relationships) in the harbor of your life because God provides a lasting and legitimate inspiration.

Think of a fresh start with God like a newly painted room. There are several benefits to reap from applying a fresh coat of paint to your home or workspace. For starters, the room looks and smells new! A new paint job typically accentuates the ambiance by making a room feel larger and more inviting. If the painting took place outside the house, the value could increase, adding curb appeal to the home.

Also, finishing a painting project gives the painter a sense of accomplishment and brings the personal perspective of a fresh new start. Likewise, a fresh start with God changes your complete outlook on everything, from your problems to your pains. Keep in mind that God is always giving us opportunities to paint (get right with Him.) Thus, we must be willing to pick up the paintbrush (the Bible) and get busy! See, Scripture contains unique "fresh start invitations" from God that we need to accept. God told His wayward people in Isaiah 1:18, *"Come now, let us reason together, says the Lord: though your sins are like scarlet, they shall be as white as snow; though they are red like crimson, they shall become like wool."*

In the New Testament, Jesus told those weighed down by their powerless religion and human-made traditions to come to Him. Matthew 11:28, Then Jesus said, *"Come to me, all of you who are weary and carry heavy burdens, and I will give you rest."*

Regardless of how dirty or damaged your walls (heart) are, God is ready for you to roll a fresh start in your life through His grace and goodness. Knowing this, accept God's invitations, which typically include repentance at times, rededication, and refocusing. The refocusing aspect should involve prayer and daily Scripture reading. These actions will position you to start fast and fresh. Therefore, whether it's the start of a new year, job, school, relationship, or another new beginning, you can start fresh with God!

Thinking About My Inspiration

Reflective thinking: A fresh start with God changes your complete outlook on everything, from your problems to your pains.

Review Verse: Isaiah 1:18 *"Come now, let us reason together, says the Lord: though your sins are like scarlet, they shall be as white as snow; though they are red like crimson, they shall become like wool."*

Responsive action: Begin my new start with prayer and daily Scripture reading.

NOTES

Keep Moving Forward No Matter What | Day 2

"The hero and the coward both feel the same thing. But the hero uses his fear, projects it onto his opponent while the coward runs." -- Cus D'amato, American Boxing Coach

"I focus on this one thing: Forgetting the past and looking forward to what lies ahead." -- Philippians 3:13 / NLT

Life is similar to a boxing match. You will get punched, pushed into a corner, and you may even get knocked down. Rocky Balboa knew what it was like to dodge punches, but he also understood how to fight back.

Balboa once said in the iconic Rocky movie franchise, *"It ain't about how hard you hit. It's about how hard you can get hit and keep moving forward."*

This New Year, you'll take your fair share of shots. Some punches will be low blows, and others will land on your chin. The key to standing strong in the fight is to keep moving. In a boxing match, foot and hand speed are essential. A fundamental tip in boxing is that it's *"harder to hit a moving target."* Spiritually the same is true. You will be a sitting duck if you are stagnant and lazy with your spiritual commitments! Remember, focusing on moving forward with patience and perseverance in the Lord's plan is essential.

Psalm 31:24 says, *"Be strong, and let your heart take courage, all you who wait for the Lord!"*

Being patient doesn't mean you do nothing. Instead, waiting on the Lord includes: fasting, prayer, serving, and worship. The combination of these spiritual actions and exercises will not only make you a more challenging target to hit, but you will also land some much-needed counterpunches. Thus, think of participating in those spiritual steps as a pounding jab. In the boxing ring, a jab is considered the most important punch. It establishes both your offense and defense as a fighter. Many trainers believe that a strong jab increases the potential for victory. Like the jab punch, you set yourself up for success when you seek God in the ways mentioned.

The Apostle Paul saw life and ministry as a fighting competition as well. First Corinthians 9:25-27a, *"All athletes are disciplined in their training. They do it to win a prize that will fade away, but we do it for an eternal prize. 26 So, I run with purpose in every step. I am not just shadowboxing. 27 I discipline my body like an athlete, training it to do what it should...."*

As you avail yourself of these spiritual disciplines, you'll be ready for any adversity. You will be prepared for those left hooks of hardship and cheap shot struggles that come your way. You will have confidence regardless of your circumstances. Never cease to keep moving forward in the growth of your faith, and don't give up! The Lord will grant you the resolve and strength you need to win, even if you have hit the mat a few times. Psalm 144:1 says, *"Praise the Lord, who is my rock. He trains my hands for war and gives my fingers skill for battle."*

Knowing this, we can share in the humble yet confident Boxer's Prayer that says: *"I ask you not for victory, for somehow that seems wrong but only for protection and courage to be strong. Strength not to conquer but just that I fight well and prove myself a sportsman at the final bell."*

Thinking About My Inspiration

Reflective thinking: In this New Year, you will take your fair share of shots. Some punches will be low blows, and others will land on your chin. The key to remaining in the fight is to keep moving.

Review Verse: Philippians 3:13, *"I focus on this one thing: Forgetting the past and looking forward to what lies ahead."*

Responsive Prayer: *"Lord, I know the left hooks of hardship, and cheap shots struggles are coming. Help me to keep moving on the path and the pace you desire!"* In Jesus' Name, Amen.

NOTES

Turn Your Resolutions Into Realities | Day 3

"The first step towards getting somewhere is to decide you're not going to stay where you are." — J.P. Morgan, Investor.

Matthew 6:33, *"Seek the Kingdom of God above all else, and live righteously, and he will give you everything you need."*

Our goals look impressive on paper, but the distance between our list of resolutions and reality is sometimes miles apart! Statistics show that plans for healthy eating and exercise fall by the wayside by the third week of January or approximately 21 days into a new program at any point of the year, along with several other meaningful objectives. See, good intentions fall short of taking you where you need to go. However, making intentional decisions about what needs to change is the key to turning those resolutions into realities.

Here are three key focal points:

Add value to others. Leadership Teacher, John Maxwell says, *"Success is when I add value to myself. Significance is when I add value to others."* So many people say they want to live a purposeful life but are too busy spending their time, money, and talents on themselves. God has planned your life for a greater mission. Ephesians 2:10, *"For we are*

God's masterpiece. He has created us anew in Christ Jesus, so we can do the good things he planned for us long ago."

Guard your time. As my friend Ken Adams says, *"If You don't tell your time where to go, someone else will do it for you."* Having a game plan for your day and week will help you be productive and reduce your stress levels. Yes, there will be some curveballs, but your ability to schedule will help protect your time. You can always make more money but you can't make more time. So you need to invest your time wisely.

Psalm 90:12 says, *"Teach us to number our days, that we may gain a heart of wisdom."*

Make God a priority. The most important relationship you foster is with God. As you go to church, get in the Bible and pray, you can expect the other areas in your life, such as your emotional, relational, and spiritual well-being, to improve. Matthew 6:33, *"Seek the Kingdom of God above all else, and live righteously, and he will give you everything you need."*

You may be wondering, *how do these steps enhance my goals and resolutions?* Think of the game of dominos. Every good decision you make in this new year will positively impact everything and everyone nearby because choices cause a chain reaction (*the domino effect.*)

Thinking About My Inspiration

Reflective Thinking: Making intentional decisions about what needs to change is the key to turning those resolutions into realities.

Review Verse: "Matthew 6:33, *"Seek the Kingdom of God above all else, and live righteously, and he will give you everything you need."*

Responsive Prayer: Lord, help me to be productive on your terms because you bless me to be a blessing.

NOTES

You're Never Too Busy To Pray | Day 4

"You can do more than pray after you have prayed, but you can not do more than pray until you have prayed." -- John Bunyan, English Writer

First Thessalonians 5:16 / ESV, *"Pray without ceasing."*

New beginnings sometimes mean increased busyness. As a result, regular practices like prayer pay the price. However, regardless of how engaged our new opportunities may make us, we must remember that we are never too busy to pray.

Certain words and writings have a way of putting everything in perspective. For me, the poem *"Too Busy To Pray"* is always a timely reminder of what matters most, and it goes like this:

One morning, I got up early and rushed right into the day! I had so much to accomplish that I didn't take the time to pray. Problems just tumbled about me, and heavier came each task. "Why doesn't God help me?" I wondered. He answered, "You didn't ask!"
I tried to come into God's presence; I used all my keys at the lock. God gently and lovingly chided, "Why, child, you didn't knock!" I wanted to see joy and beauty, but the day toiled on, gray and bleak. I wondered why God didn't show me. He answered me, "But you didn't seek." I woke

up early the next morning and paused before entering the day. I had so much to accomplish that I had to take time to pray.

I often think that the author remains *anonymous* because this type of poetry must have dropped straight down from heaven so that everyone could refocus on meeting with God first thing in the morning. *Psalm 63:1* says, *"O GOD, You are my God; Early will I seek You"*

The practice of meeting early with our heavenly Father is something Jesus personified as well. Mark 1:35 says, *"Very early in the morning, while it was still dark, Jesus got up, left the house, and went off to a solitary place, where he prayed."*

Even people who require less sleep still need to get their rest. Thus, regardless of the Lord's bedtime, He made an early morning meeting with His Father a priority, and so should we! He also made it a point to get alone with His Father. Finding alone time is one of the more challenging factors in being faithful in meeting with God. Thus, the early part of the day is the most valuable and productive time to meet with God before the hustle and bustle begin. Notice that when Jesus arrived at his solitary place, he prayed. We should emulate His plan and seek to communicate with Him daily.

Ultimately, when we choose to be intentional about meeting God in the morning, there will be movement in our lives like never before. Therefore, start your year or new opportunity *with* prayer!

Thinking About My Inspiration

Reflective Thinking: "Test what you hear by seeking truth from God's Word."

Review Verse: I Thessalonians 5:16, *"Pray without ceasing."*

Responsive Prayer: "*My Father in heaven, remind me often how I need to connect with you in prayer.*"

NOTES

New Year's Preparation | Day 5

"By failing to prepare, you are preparing to fail" -- Benjamin Franklin, American author, scientist, and Statesman.

Proverbs 24:27 *"Do your planning and prepare your fields before building your house."*

Approximately tens of thousands of people each year jam the Time Square area in New York to ring in the New Year. To accommodate crowd safety in 2020, newly appointed Counter-Terrorism Chief of the NYPD, Martine Materasso, said the department planned this event all year. Those preparations included a significant show of force by the New York Police Department with uniform personnel. Also, two kinds of bomb-sniffing dogs were on hand: Special Labradors, known as Vapor Wake Sniffing Dogs trained to search out people wearing body explosives, and K9- Shepherd bomb-sniffing dogs used for detecting more traditional bombs. John Miller, NYPD Deputy Commissioner of Intelligence and Counterterrorism, said, *"While there is no imminent threat, Times Square will be the safest place on earth."*

As you approach this new year, consider taking similar precautions in your planning.

Proverbs 22:3 says, *"A prudent person foresees danger and takes precautions. The simpleton goes blindly on and suffers the consequences."*

Over the next *12* months, you can expect temptation, trials, and troubles to attack you without warning. Preparing yourself spiritually, emotionally, relationally, and financially is wise and crucial. Many terrorist plots are foiled and never make the news because of the preparedness of our law enforcement. Likewise, your preparation for the new year is essential! You can prepare yourself for the new year by attending church, small groups, prayer meetings, and Bible classes. The commitment you make to God will significantly strengthen your connection to Him.

Another reason to be prepared is that it equips you to share your faith. People will challenge and even ridicule the mentioned Christ- centered commitments. 1 Peter 3:15 says, *"...but in your hearts honor Christ the Lord as holy, always being prepared to make a defense to anyone who asks you for a reason for the hope that is in you; yet do it with gentleness and respect..."*

Remember, *preparation* is the breakfast of champions. We are less scared when prepared. As you ready yourself and implement these plans, you can expect to reap a harvest of growth and strength. Spiritual preparation will always produce spiritual gains in your life.

By God's power and your preparation, the new year can be a milestone time of growth for you!

Thinking About My Inspiration

Reflective Thinking: Approach the new year with preparation in mind.

Review Verse: Proverbs 24:27, *"Do your planning and prepare your fields before building your house. Life and death lie in the power of a tongue."Amen*

Responsive Prayer: Lord, lead my heart and mind to be diligent in *preparation* so I can pursue excellence in everything I do. Amen.

NOTES

Get On The Right Path | Day 6

"Mark out a straight path for your feet; stay on the safe path. Don't get sidetracked; keep your feet from following evil." -King Solomon

Psalm 119:105 / NLT: *"Your word is a lamp to guide my feet and a light for my path."*

A man was watching the news one night, which reported that a car was going in the wrong direction on the freeway. The man knew his wife was on that freeway and became very concerned, so he called her on her cell phone. She answered, and he said, *"Dear, there's one car going in the wrong direction on the freeway."* She exclaimed, *"One car? There are hundreds of them!"*

Maybe you can relate? Perhaps last year, you spent some time going in the wrong direction. As a result, those unfriendly feelings of guilt and regret were flying at you like cars on the freeway! Therefore, with a fresh new year in session, consider going in the right direction. Before stressing over how you will do this, remember that God promises His support. Psalm 16:11 says, *"You make known to me the path of life; in your presence, there is fullness of joy; at your right hand are pleasures forevermore."*

And in Psalm 32:8, God declares, *"I will instruct you and teach you in the way you should go; I will counsel you with my loving eye on you."*

As you seek God, He will reveal His plans and path for you. You see, the turn of a calendar year provides a unique opportunity to make these adjustments. Thus staying in the wrong lane and going in the wrong direction is foolishness when you consider God's forgiveness and faithfulness. He desires to rain His blessings, but we must be willing to go in His order. If you are having trouble getting on the right path, take some time to reflect on the 2005 hit song *'Jesus Take the Wheel'* performed by Carrie Underwood. Part of the chorus says, *"Jesus, take the wheel, Take it from my hands 'Cause I can't do this on my own, I'm letting go..."*

To get on the right path this year, you will need to let go! Let go of your *"know-it-all attitude"* and those selfish actions. Surrendering control is never easy, but it's hard not to see the blessing in doing it. Let it go and lean on the Lord. Proverbs 3:5-6 says, *"Trust in the Lord, with all your heart, and do not lean on your own understanding. In all your ways, acknowledge him, and he will make straight your paths."*

Thinking About My Inspiration

Reflective Thinking: *"Before you begin to stress over how you're going to do this, remember that God promises His support."*

Review Verse: Psalm 119:105 / ESV, *"Your word is a lamp to guide my feet and a light for my path."*

Responsive Prayer: Lord, direct my steps and push me toward the path that you approve of for me. Amen

NOTES

Lose The Weight of People's Opinions | Day 7

"Stop allowing negative people and their words to control your life." -- Anonymous

Proverbs 18:21 / EHV, *"Life and death lie in the power of a tongue."*

According to sources like *Yougove.com*, nearly half of all resolutions made at the beginning of the year and other new entry points have to do with weight loss.

So, in addition to shedding a few unnecessary pounds, consider losing the unsolicited opinions of others that are agenda driven. See, the poundage of unproductive views of others goes to our minds, not our midsection. Consequently, we become socially sluggish and emotionally blotted with insecurity. Thus, we need to restrict those unhealthy mental calories from opinionated people who only look to spread discouragement and toxic thoughts. Sadly, some find their worth in trying to bring down your value with their unkind vocabulary.

Ultimately, poisonous opinions come from a contaminated heart. In Luke 6:45, Jesus said, *"The good person out of the good treasure ofhis heart produces good, and the evil person out of his evil treasureproduces evil, for out of the abundance of the heart his mouth speaks."* Scripture makes it clear not to listen to such nonsense.

Psalm 1:1 says, *"Blessed is the man who walks not in the counsel of the wicked..."*

There is significant value in getting counsel, but there is a difference between trustworthy advice and careless views, especially when those assertions come with a motivation to break and bring you down. In the big picture, you live to the audience of one. Unkind and harmful remarks and discouraging talk will fly your way like heat-seeking missiles. These words of destruction will sometimes come from trusted sources like doctors, teachers, and even pastors but remember, God has the best and final say. Proverbs 16:1 says, *"We humans make plans, but the Lord has the final word."*

With this in mind, impose upon your thoughts a *faith filter*: First, test what you hear by seeking truth from God's Word. Ask yourself if what you hear lines up with Scripture. Secondly, refuse let opinions based on someone else's issues control you any longer.

As you walk in the certainty of Scripture and apply the guidance you get, pass it on to those who ask for your help. This perspective will help you get off to a good start and remain on the path God has for you!

Thinking About My Inspiration

Reflective Thinking: "Test what you hear by seeking truth from God's Word."

Review Verse: Proverbs 18:21, *"Life and death lie in the power of a tongue..."*

Responsive Prayer: "Lord, help me to rise above discouragement and weigh the words I hear against your Word."

NOTES

God Has New Ground For You | Day 8

"Take the first step in faith. You don't have to see the whole staircase, just take the first step." -- Martin Luther King Jr. Preacher, Civil Rights Leader

Proverbs 3:5-6 / CSB, *"Trust in the Lord with all your heart, and do not rely on your own understanding; 6 in all your ways know him, and he will make your paths straight."*

Christoper Columbus is best known for being an Italian-born explorer who historically landed in the Bahamas, becoming the first European to explore the Americas since the early Vikings. In 1937, Columbus Day became a federally recognized holiday when President Franklin D. Roosevelt gave it proclamation status. Since then, events such as parades and religious ceremonies have been organized to acknowledge Christoper Columbus' explorations and his Italian heritage.

While you may not have command of the Nina, Pinta, and Santa Maria ships, God has called you to explore and take new ground in this life. Scripture provides examples of this perspective. For instance, in Genesis 13:17, God told Abram to take new ground. *"Go, walk through the length and breadth of the land, for I am giving it to you."* Another memorable directive is given to Joshua in Joshua 1:11: *"Go through the camp and tell the people to get their provisions ready. In three days, you will cross the Jordan River and take possession of the land the Lord your God is giving you."*

Knowing this, you can pray for God to expand your borders. Whether with business, finances, or responsibilities, ask God to bless you so you can be a blessing to His Kingdom work. A man named Jabez prayed a similar prayer in First Chronicles 4:9-10 which says, *"There was a man named Jabez who was more honorable than any of his brothers. His mother named him Jabez because his birth had been so painful. 10 He was the one who prayed to the God of Israel, "Oh, that you would bless me and expand my territory!"*

You can also prayerfully seek God for higher ground with your integrity, purity, and humility. You don't have to stay where you are; God's will is that you would grow in the grace and truth of His Word. Praying and believing this way requires an adventurous spirit seeking the higher ground of God.

A chorus from the *1892* hymn Higher Ground says it all: *"Lord, lift me up and let me stand, By faith on Heaven's table land.*

A higher plane than I have found, Lord, plant my feet on higher ground."

Thinking About My Inspiration

Reflective Thinking: *"Take that first step of faith."*

Review Verse: Proverbs 3:5-6 / CSB *"Trust in the Lord with all your heart, and do not rely on your own understanding; 6 in all your ways know him, and he will make your paths straight."*

Responsive Prayer: Lord, thank you for giving me the strength to step forward in faith." Amen

NOTES

Praying For Discernment | Day 9

"Discernment is God's call to intercession, never to fault-finding." — Corrie ten Boom

Proverbs 3:21 / NLT, *"My child, don't lose sight of common sense and discernment. Hang on to them."*

Neurological studies reveal that our brains can process approximately *11 million bits of information* every second! Even in an unconscious state, our minds can handle between 40-50 bits of data per second. Thus, it should be no surprise that the Bible instructs its readers to seek God for discernment prayerfully. Psalm 119:169 says, *"O Lord, listen to my cry; give me the discerning mind you promised."*

Discernment can be understood as the indispensable ability to think and act Biblically about all decisions. Thankfully, we can prayerfully ask God to provide a discerning mind so we can meet the moment of decision and the uncertainties of this upcoming year. See, whether it is professional choices about your career and education or personal decisions about faith and family, you need the blessing of discernment so you can respond productively and wisely.

Also, discernment helps us to distinguish between sound teaching from God's Word and false teaching. Likewise, it provides conviction on what is good versus what is evil.

Therefore, the Scripture tells us to examine everything, and discernment plays a significant role in that approach. First, Thessalonians 5:21-22 says, *"but test everything that is said. Hold on to what is good. 22 Stay away from every kind of evil."* When we take time to ask God for discernment, we are essentially asking God for His guidance and insight from His Word. Remember that God's Holy standards, thoughts, and ways are not ours. Isaiah 55:8 says, *"My plans aren't your plans, nor are your ways my ways, says the Lord."*

Knowing this, we can't fall into the trap of chasing our feelings. Instead, we need a discerning mind of faith that seeks to lean on the Spirit for correction and to trust God's leading. When we pray and share this perspective of discernment, we will honor God, clear away distractions, and realize our potential in Christ. Philippians 1:9-10 tells us, *"And it is my prayer that your love may abound more and more, with knowledge and all discernment, so that you may approve what is excellent, and so be pure and blameless for the day of Christ."*

Thinking About My Inspiration

Reflective Thinking: *"We can prayerfully ask God to provide a discerning mind so we can meet the moment of decision and the uncertainties of this upcoming year."*

Review Verse: Proverbs 3:21 / NLT, *"My child, don't lose sight of common sense and discernment. Hang on to them."*

Responsive Prayer: "Lord, grant me a discerning mind so that I can honor you and help advance your kingdom purposes." Amen

NOTES

"Hard work beats talent when talent doesn't work hard." — Tim Notke, Basketball Coach

Proverbs 12:11 / NLT, *"A hard worker has plenty of food, but a person who chases fantasies has no sense."*

I once read that Spanish composer-cellist *Pablo Casals* was in the final years of his life when a young reporter asked him, *"Mr. Casals, you are ninety-five years old and the greatest cellist that ever lived. Why do you still practice six hours a day?"*

What was Casals's answer? *"Because I think I'm making progress,"* he said. You may not be a cellist like Casals, but you sure can emulate his work ethic. Your spiritual growth is no different. See some people think that their walk with God is truly on autopilot with little to no responsibility to progress, but that is not accurate. Dedication to continued growth leads to success in everything, especially faith. A good time to put extra effort into your spiritual growth is at the start of a new year or season in your life. Mentally you are locked in and devoted to putting in the work for change.

Philippians 2:12 says, *"Therefore, my beloved, as you have always obeyed, so now, not only as in my presence but much more in my absence, work out your own salvation with fear and trembling."*

The phrase in the Greek manuscript conveys the idea of *"carrying out"* something. In this case, the focus is carrying out your responsibility to grow spiritually. See, we need to focus on *"working out"* what God has worked in each of us through Christ. Like mining, we need to dig deep to find the "motherload" of growth that God has for us.

Remember, *"surface-seeking"* will never yield spiritual maturity. Ultimately, we are as close to God as we choose to be. Paul's mention of *"fear and trembling"* refers to having a deep reverence for God, which should motivate us. Thus, praying, reading Scripture, church attendance, Bible studies, serving, and giving are ways to work out our salvation tangibly. We need to practice these spiritual disciplines and repeat them daily if we want to grow.

Thinking About My Inspiration

Reflective Thinking: *"Dedication to continued growth leads to success in everything, especially faith."*

Review Verse: Proverbs 12:11 / NLT, *"A hard worker has plenty of food, but a person who chases fantasies has no sense."*

Responsive Prayer: "Lord, there is fullness in your promises and presence. Lead me each day to seek you and read your Word." Amen

NOTES

44

Treat People Right | Day 11

"I follow three rules: Do the right thing, do the best you can, and always show people you care." -- Lou Holtz, College Football Coach

Luke 6:37 / NLT *"Do not judge others, and you will not be judged. Do not condemn others, or it will all come back against you. Forgive others, and you will be forgiven."*

Whether we realize it or not, happiness is tied to our harmony with others. When we are in a constant state of conflict, contentment becomes elusive. Thus, if we lack respect and treat the people around us harshly and unfairly, our attitude will dip even more.

See, maturity shows up in relationships; how we treat others matters to God and should matter to us. Perhaps as we begin a new year, the value of *"Treating Others Right"* can become our guiding light. To help us with this critical responsibility, Jesus gave us the Golden Rule: *"In everything, treat others as you would want them to treat you, for this fulfills the law and the prophets"* (Matthew 7:12.)

Interestingly, a version of the Golden Rule appears in many world religions and cultures. Albeit, the Bible's presentation of the Golden Rule is the most accurate regarding selflessness and sincerity.

Whether it's the Bible or a religious document, it is universally acceptable to treat people right. But if you're still not convinced that this is important, take the common sense approach. Imagine saying to someone, *"Can you please treat me worse than I treat you?"* You will not find anyone saying that because everyone wants fair treatment.

See the Golden Rule ensures that you will be ethical and show integrity with others. Sometimes in life, doing what is right and treating others right will not be a popular decision. In some cases, it may prove costly in terms of patience, pride, or popularity. The Josephson Institute of Ethics observed, *"Ethics is about how we meet the challenge of doing the right thing when that will cost more than we want to pay."*

The Golden Rule helps eliminate any wavering concerning ethical decisions with people. As you seek to treat people right, a common ground of respect is many times reciprocated.

Also, approaching relationships this way doesn't mean you will see eye to eye with everyone. Instead, the Golden Rule allows you to disagree with others while not being disagreeable in your behavior. To be disagreeable is the equivalent of being offensive, prideful, rude, or obnoxious. Whereas respectfully disagreeing maintains the connection regardless of how far apart your views may be.

Remember, we've all blown it when it comes to treating people right! Therefore, we need to be purposeful in how we act and respond.

Thankfully God offers forgiveness and this golden guideline for future success. Therefore, apply God's standard and pray for the will to follow it.

Thinking About My Inspiration

Reflective Thinking: *"Dedication to continued growth leads to success in everything, especially faith."*

Review Verse: Luke 6:37 / NLT, *"Do not judge others, and you will not be judged. Do not condemn others, or it will all come back against you. Forgive others, and you will be forgiven."*

Responsive Prayer: "May my attitudes and actions be a blessing not a burden to others." Amen

NOTES

Push Against Your Problems | Day 12

"To be a Christian without prayer is no more possible than to be alive without breathing." - Martin Luther

James 5:16 / TLB, *"Admit your faults to one another and pray for each other so that you may be healed. The earnest prayer of a righteous man has great power and wonderful results."*

Even though the calendar year may have turned or a new season in your life has begun, you will soon notice that life's problems are relentless. Problems are like bullies; they like to push you around but don't like it when you push back! So when issues come your way, you need to first take them from "me to we"—that's called prayer. The next step found in the Scriptures is to ramp up your prayer life by making it persistent. Constant communication with God takes your prayers and relationship with Him to another level.

Luke 18 introduces us to a woman who is in a desperate situation. She was the victim of manipulation, thereby losing land and livestock. With no male representation or family assistance to note, she persistently went before the judge in her region. Sadly enough, the judge was a man with no regard for God or respect for people— a terrible combination! Staying true to his character, he ignored the woman's request for justice.

Verses 2-3 of Luke 18 says, *"There was a judge in a certain town who didn't fear God or respect people. 3 And a widow in that town kept coming to him, saying, 'Give me justice against my adversary."*

Problems can be draining and dangerous. If you're not careful, they can lead you to depression. The only way to overcome this discouragement is to push back with persistence. The lonely widow did just that! PUSH can be understood as *PRAY UNTIL SOMETHING HAPPENS*. The parable reveals that the widow kept coming. Her tenacity is something that is commonly attached to the encouragement of prayer. Ephesians 6:18 says, *"Pray in the Spirit at all times and on every occasion. Stay alert and be persistent in your prayers for all believers everywhere."*

If you have a problem right now, you are a candidate for a miracle! As you persistently seek God, He will faithfully close or open doors that lead to your provision. While it may sound simple, the fact is that when we are in the midst of a storm, we usually run away from God instead of running to Him. The enemy likes to pound us with doubt and disconnection when we are down. As a result, you may pull away from the Lord. Thus, the strategy to push against the problem with persistence is what you need to do.

By God's grace, you will keep on pushing. Don't give up before the miracle!

Thinking About My Inspiration

Reflective Thinking: "Constant communication with God takes your prayers and relationship with Him to another level."

Review Verse: James 5:16 / TLB, *"Admit your faults to one another and pray for each other so that you may be healed. The earnest prayer of a righteous man has great power and wonderful results."*

Responsive Prayer: "Give me this day, my daily bread." Amen

NOTES

Sincere Confession | Day 13

"The confession of evil works is the first beginning of good works." - Saint Augustine

First John 1:9 / NIV, *"If we confess our sins, he is faithful and just and will forgive us our sins and purify us from all unrighteousness."*

It's possible to read the Bible, pray, attend church, sing the songs, volunteer, and give, yet miss the command to do all those noble acts with authenticity. In the Old Testament, God rejected offerings, worship, and feasts that lacked sincerity.

Likewise, in the New Testament, Jesus taught that giving, praying, or fasting void of genuineness was essentially worthless. The practice of confession is no different. The way forward after a sinful failure of any kind is heartfelt admission. To help understand this point, consider viewing confession through the legal lens of law. In court proceedings, confession is agreeing that you are culpable of a crime or misconduct that broke the law. Thus confession is an admission of guilt and an attitude that agrees with God over sin.

Knowing this, we must be honest and humble about our shortcomings and sins because failure to do so only prolongs the bondage!

A story that puts this into perspective is that of the Prussian king, *Frederick the Great*, who was once touring a Berlin prison. The prisoners fell on their knees before him to proclaim their innocence -- except for one man, who remained silent.

Frederick called to him, *"Why are you here?"* "Armed robbery, Your Majesty," was the reply. "And are you guilty?" *"Yes indeed, Your Majesty, I deserve my punishment."* Frederick then summoned the jailer and ordered him, *"Release this guilty wretch at once. I will not keep him in this prison where he will corrupt all the fine innocent people who occupy it!"*

Like this unpretentious prisoner, we need to seek God's mercy by sincerely fessing up about our sins. In Psalm 32:-3-5 David wrote, *"When I refused to confess my sin, my body wasted away, and I groaned all day long. 4 Day and night, your hand of discipline was heavy on me. My strength evaporated like water in the summer heat. Interlude 5 Finally, I confessed all my sins to you and stopped trying to hide my guilt. I said to myself, "I will confess my rebellion to the Lord." And you forgave me! All my guilt is gone."*

See, confession is a vital component of your faith and overall ability to have, as they say, *"A Happy and healthy New Year."* However, you will be hard-pressed to find happiness and health without confession. Thankfully, God has built within us the capability to experience conviction over wrongdoing, and by His grace, we have the opportunity to get right with Him through sincere confession!

Thinking About My Inspiration

Reflective Thinking: *"We must be honest and humble about our shortcomings and sins because failure to do so only prolongs the bondage!"*

Review Verse: First John 1:9 / NIV, *"If we confess our sins, he is faithful and just and will forgive us our sins and purify us from all unrighteousness."*

Responsive Prayer: "My Father and my God, I confess my sinful actions and attitudes before you. Convict me of anything else I am missing, and be merciful to me, my Lord!" Amen

NOTES

God Buries Your Sins In The Sea | Day 14

"Forgiveness is the divine miracle of grace." -- Oswald Chambers

"And I will be merciful to them in their wrongdoings, and I will remember their sins no more." -- Hebrews 8:12 / TLB

Mariana Trench, the crescent-shaped channel in the Western Pacific, is located east of the Mariana Islands near Guam. It is home to what is regarded by ocean explorers as the deepest part of the ocean, touching down at an impressive *36,070* feet below sea level. By comparison, the indomitable Mount Everest stands at a staggering *29,026* feet above sea level. The deepest part of the Mariana Trench is *7,044* feet deeper than Everest's height!

When God created the Mariana Trench, He illustrated the depths of His compassion and forgiveness. Micah 7:19 says, *"Once again, you will have compassion on us. You will trample our sins under your feet and throw them into the depths of the ocean!"*

Often, fear and false guilt cause you to think that God throws you into the ocean's depths, not your sin! Thankfully that is not the case. Instead, He lovingly casts your sins into the *"Sea of Forgetfulness."* When you accept the perfect sacrifice of His Son on the cross, God considers your sin *"out-of-sight and out-of-mind."* The entire purpose of God's provision of His Son exemplifies His unmerited favor and mercy. John 3:17 says, *"For God did not send his Son into the world to condemn the world, but to save the world through him."*

As you enter a new year, you will still face those old foes of regret and shame. Your ability to reach your resolutions and fulfill your purpose is primarily connected to your emotional health. Thus, if you're living in a constant state of guilt, you will become unhealthy and distracted, and sadly, it will be impossible to take the new ground that God has for you this year.

The key, then, is to rest in His blessing of forgiveness. Rather than beating yourself up with more guilt or pity parties, take God at His Word. Romans 8:1 says, *"So now there is no condemnation for those who belong to Christ Jesus."*

Missionary *Corrie ten Boom* once shared, *"God buries our sins in the depths of the sea and then posts up a sign that reads, "No fishing."*

Knowing this, stop fishing for your failures because God has graciously forgiven you. Focus now on *"finishing well"* the assignments and opportunities our Lord has given you.

Thinking About My Inspiration

Reflective Thinking: *"He lovingly casts your sins into the "Sea of Forgetfulness."*

Review Verse: Hebrews 8:12 / TLB, *"And I will be merciful to them in their wrongdoings, and I will remember their sins no more."*

Responsive Prayer: *"Thank you, Lord, for your mercy and forgiveness. Remind me of your grace when false guilt tries to get me down."* In Jesus' Name, Amen

Take Your Troubles To God | Day 15

"I've heard there are troubles of more than one kind; some come from ahead, and some come from behind. But I've brought a big bat. I'm all ready, you see; now my troubles are going to have troubles with me!" — Dr. Seuss

"Let not your hearts be troubled. Believe in God; believe also in me." -- John 14:1

Studies conducted at New York University found that the honeymoon stage for marriage is approximately thirty months. Likewise, periods of bliss over a new job last about six months, and a new school semester is even shorter, coming in at around four weeks! The same is said for a new year or new season. After these periods, the bloom is off the rose, and problems begin and become more visible. When this happens, you need a strategy to deal effectively with your situation.

See, everyone processes their troubles differently. Some blow up and get angry, while others clam up and withdraw. Other common reactions include complaining, rash replies, intense fear, irritation, overwhelming anxiety, and the temptation to numb the stress with a sinful vice. Although these responses are diverse, they all share the same unproductive results. Thus, when it comes to your troubles, you need to take them to God before they take you down!

Psalm 120:1 says, *"I took my troubles to the Lord; I cried out to him, and he answered my prayer."*

When tussling with your troubles, a wise and effective strategy is to talk with God. Notice the Psalmist made an effort to bring his burdens before the Lord. His prayer was passionate and sincere, yielding an answer from God. We often treat God as a fallback option or plan b or c, but we must seek Him first when the fight becomes real. Perhaps the hesitation is pride in thinking we can manage our madness alone, or it's poor planning and distracted living. Whatever the reasoning, we must remember that prayer is indeed powerful and our best recourse when the struggles of life come.

John Bunyan, the author of Pilgrim's Progress, understood this, and he once said, *"You can do more than pray after you have prayed, but you cannot do more than pray until you have prayed. Pray often, for prayer is a shield to the soul, a sacrifice to God, and a scourge to Satan."*

Knowing this, let us pray about those big troubles and even our pesky problems. Equally important is the perspective that says I will no longer procrastinate with prayer because God is my place of refuge and strength. Psalm 46:1 reminds us, *"God is our refuge and strength, always ready to help in times of trouble."*

Thinking About My Inspiration

Reflective Thinking: "When it comes to your troubles, you need to take them to God before they take you down!"

Review Verse: John 14:1, *"Let not your hearts be troubled. Believe in God; believe also in me."*

Responsive Prayer: "Oh God I bring my troubles before you. Be my refuge and strength in this, my time of need."

NOTES

Thinking About Your Choices | Day 16

"Thinking is hard work; that's why so few do it." -- Albert Einstein, Nobel Prize-Winning Physicist

"When I think on my ways, I turn my feet to your testimonies." -- Psalm 119:59 / ESV

Being a person of faith doesn't mean you're an airhead. Nor do the Scriptures call you to leave life's matters to chance. Instead, God desires that you use the mind He gave you to think in productive and prudent ways. Proverbs 13:18 says, *"Wise people think before they act; fools don't—and even brag about their foolishness."*

Whenever you make the time to think about your choices, you are revealing maturity and wisdom. The Bible declares that it's utter foolishness to do otherwise.

Taking time to think about your decisions provides opportunities for prayer and support. You are more likely to pray about problems or responsibilities when you think about them first. However, when you rush from one area of life to another, stress and worry dominate your thoughts. As a result, hasty decisions are made, and sometimes irreversible acts are put into play. Thinking and praying before making decisions will always prove to be an indispensable combination. This practice of *"thinking first"* is especially beneficial at the start of a new year or opportunity. You can think through your health, schedule, goals, resolutions, relationships, and more. You will find that this approach will help reduce stress and increase your effectiveness.

Also, thinking allows you the opportunity to gather valuable input from others. Proverbs 12:15 says, *"The way of a fool is right in his own eyes, but a wise man listens to advice."* It's hard to stop and request guidance if you're always going 100 MPH. Taking time to think about your circumstances will bring to mind people that can help. Typically you want to lean on those with experience and a godly character. Their words and counsel will provide you with perspectives that are sometimes hard to reach on your own. This approach will help you with many areas, such as finances, parenting, relationships, spiritual walk, etc.

Thinking about situations and seeking God and trusted sources will always invite God's blessing. Humility and a teachable attitude will undoubtedly lead to God's approval.

Thinking About My Inspiration

Reflective Thinking: *"Test what you hear by seeking truth from God's Word. Taking time to think about your decisions provides opportunities for prayer and support."*

Review Verse: Psalm 119:59 / ESV, *"When I think on my ways, I turn my feet to your testimonies."*

Responsive Prayer: "Lord, I commit my mind to you. Help me to think about your testimonies and to take the path you provide. Guide my thoughts and actions."

NOTES

Focus On Being Teachable | Day 17

"Be teachable; you are not always right." – Unknown

Psalm 86:11 / NLT: "Teach me your ways, O Lord, that I may live according to your truth! Grant me purity of heart, so that I may honor you."

As a new year begins, you will likely implement healthy choices that will hopefully yield profitable returns. However, the key to success goes far deeper than your capability or willpower. See, the ability to advance past adversity and reach your desired achievements comes down to you being teachable. Let's face it, we can accomplish much in our strength, but we've seen this movie before. Eventually, we fall flat on our faces because we did it our way. Thus, the key is to be teachable before God, particularly with a good attitude.

Psalm 25:4-5 says, *"Make me to know your ways, O Lord; teach me your paths. 5 Lead me in your truth and teach me, for you are the God of my salvation; for you, I wait all the day long."*

If you possess a teachable attitude, then positive returns of learning and applying will undoubtedly follow you. However, the opposite is sadly true. If you lack a teachable attitude, you will surely miss out on many vital lessons and never reach your potential. You will also forfeit those pathways of blessing that the Psalmist mentioned.

After many years, psychologist Dr. Scott Baker learned from teaching martial arts that being teachable is critical. He said that *"a student's attitude is the most significant aspect of their nature which contributes to their success or failure in learning this complex system of skills. Attitude impacts a student's success more than natural ability and physical capacity. One can build capacity and endurance and teach skills and abilities even to the untalented, but one cannot teach the un-teachable!"*

Likewise, your attitude matters to your overall growth, success, and ability to be teachable. Remember, you will never regret being teachable before God, His Word, and His approved leaders. So take the path of being teachable, and blessings will follow!

Reflective Thinking: "The ability to advance past adversity and reach your desired achievements comes down to you being teachable."

Review Verse: Psalm 86:11 / NLT *"Teach me your ways, O Lord, that I may live according to your truth! Grant me purity of heart so that I may honor you."*

Responsive Prayer: "Lord, teach me your ways that I may honor you and be helpful to your kingdom plans."

NOTES

Wisdom Prevents Foolishness | Day 18

"Knowledge is flour, but wisdom is bread." -- AUSTIN O'MALLEY, Ophthalmologist and English Author

"If any of you lacks wisdom, you should ask God, who gives generously to all without finding fault, and it will be given to you." - - James 1:5 / ESV

A man was getting his caricature picture done—once the artist finished, the man took off with the artist's bag of money with a smirk. However, he left behind the picture of his drawing, which led to his arrest for the robbery.

While the theft showed risk, it also revealed his foolishness. Likewise, wisdom is not on your side when you're practicing dishonesty. You may think you are cunning, but foolish choices can catch up with you. Just think about some of your goals when you start something fresh, like a job, semester, or new year. Many resolutions are connected to our foolish mistakes in the previous year or setting. We say things like, *"I am going to do this differently, or I will wait for that or say this?"* Thankfully, God provides trustworthy counsel that says in Proverbs 10:23, *"Doing wrong is like a joke to a fool, but wisdom is a pleasure to a man of understanding."*

You can seek after God's wisdom through the Scriptures, prayer, godly leaders, and church. Perhaps the mode of understanding that flies under the radar for most people is the "fear of the Lord." To fear God is a high form of reverence for Him. On a human relational level, it's similar to the respect you would show a parent or grandparent. Psalm 111:10 says, *"The fear of the LORD is the beginning of wisdom; all those who practice it have a good understanding. His praise endures forever!"*

Sadly, our society looks down on God's wisdom. Some blame falls on those who proclaim themselves as Christians—but are terrible examples of Christ's love and mercy. However, at the heart of every sinful person is the fleshly desire to be rebellious toward God's counsel. Thus, in their minds, the message of the Lord and His wisdom is nothing more than foolishness.

In First Corinthians 1:18, the Apostle Paul said, *"For the message of the cross is foolishness to those who are perishing, but to us who are being saved, it is the power of God."*

The most remarkable example of wisdom is the message of the cross. There, the truth of God's perfect atoning sacrifice is displayed for all to see. Therefore, it would be best if you choose to pursue God's wisdom for those tough decisions and those struggles with temptations. God's wisdom will always keep you from foolishness and provide a powerful sense of His presence when seeking wisdom is your objective.

Thinking About My Inspiration

Reflective Thinking: *"You can seek after God's wisdom through the Scriptures, prayer, godly leaders, and church."*

Review Verse: James 1:5, *"If any of you lacks wisdom, you should ask God, who gives generously to all without finding fault, and it will be given to you."*

Responsive Prayer: "Lord, remind me to seek you're wisdom so that I can avoid making foolish decisions."

NOTES

Clichés Never Produce Change | Day 19

Talk is cheap. It is the way we organize and use our lives every day that tell what we believe in." -- Cesar Chavez, American Labor Leader

"Talk is cheap, like daydreams and other useless activities. Fear God instead." -- *Ecclesiastes 5:7 / NLT*

With the turn of the calendar year comes the avalanche of motivational clichés. Catchy slogans, commercials, and hashtags about health are hard to miss. However, these well-intended points of inspiration hardly work. The reason is that clichés never produce lasting change. Even internal mottos about physical exercise, proper nutrition, financial security, relational peace, and spiritual connectivity are not enough. Ultimately, tough talk about transformation is cheap, but it can prove costly because you never reach your goals that way. With this approach, you can potentially waste time, money, and effort. Therefore, you must become a person who takes the following actions: Begin by recognizing God as the source of legitimate and lasting change. Second Corinthians 5:17 says, *"Therefore if anyone is in Christ, he is a new creation. The old has passed away; behold, the new has come."* Long before transcendental meditation and yoga existed, there was God's plan of internal transformation. This process of change involves coming to Christ. The power behind any significant life change is Christ. The same way God breaks the hold of sin and death is the same way He helps you overcome those unhealthy habits. The key to anchoring your life and goals is to have the conviction that God is the originator of change, thus the need to depend on Him.

Choose to be healthy for righteous reasons. For example, losing weight or eating right for self-esteem isn't necessarily a wrong focus; it just is not the best one. Likewise, making changes to have a better body or more money can be good, but the focus needs to be higher. The fact is that whatever area of health you are looking to achieve, make sure that you're doing it for the glory of God. Psalm 34:2 says, *"My soul makes its boast in the LORD; let the humble hear and be glad."*

Your life, body, relationships, and finances belong to God. You are the manager of all He has entrusted to you. Knowing that God owns it all will keep you humble. Often people get healthy in an area of their life and then look down upon others that haven't reached their goals. A heart of humility follows whenever we make God the reason for our health. Your spiritual intention prevents newfound health from being a selfish tool of judgment or, worse, a platform for more sin. To God be the glory for another year, a fresh start, or a new opportunity. May His purpose be our focus.

Thinking About My Inspiration

Reflective Thinking: *"Talk is cheap, take action and leave the results to God."*

Review Verse: *Ecclesiastes 5:7, "Talk is cheap, like daydreams and other useless activities. Fear God instead."*

Responsive Prayer: *"Lord, help me to refocus on fulfilling your purposes."*

NOTES

Change Your Attitude | Day 20

"Our attitude determines our approach to life." -- John C. Maxwell, Leadership Author and Speaker

"Adopt the same attitude as that of Christ Jesus." -- Philippians 2:5 / CSB

Ellipticals, cycles, treadmills, specialized dieting, and customized workouts can yield impressive results, especially at the start of a new year. However, if you want to sustain a healthier version of yourself, you need to change how you think.

Likewise, if you desire to be stronger spiritually, emotionally, and relationally there needs to be a change in your overall attitude. See, your mood will determine how you view and value every situation, good or bad." Ephesians 4:21-23 says, *"Since you have heard about Jesus and have learned the truth that comes from him, 22 throw off your old sinful nature and your former way of life, which is corrupted by lust and deception. 23 Instead, let the Spirit renew your thoughts and attitudes. 24 Put on your new nature, created to be like God— truly righteous and holy."*

As much as it may pain you to admit it, some of your deficiencies in life come back to either apathy or a poor attitude. The only hope for transformation is the Spirit's help. You need the Holy Spirit to change your perspective.

Even if you have mental or emotional struggles from prior choices that were unhealthy, by God's grace, His Spirit can change you. The Spirit's miracle-working power is your only shot at lasting and legitimate success. Thus, you will need the Spirit's touch to dismantle the old you and transform you into the new you. Keep in mind that this change is not void of your efforts. This process requires prayer, repentance, surrender, and obedience for change to be possible. Also, surrounding yourself with the right support system in the form of accountability and wise friends that know the Lord will only increase the speed of your change.

Getting rid of our old habits is no easy task, but it is possible with the Spirit's leading. Be patient and prudent with your next steps. God will work on you as you are faithful to trust Him.

Reflective Thinking: *"Your attitude will determine how you view and value every situation, good or bad."*

Review Verse: Philippians 2:5, *"Adopt the same attitude as that of Christ Jesus."*

Responsive Prayer: *"Examine my attitude and point out anything that offends You."*

NOTES

Hydrate Your Soul | Day 21

"Drink a lot of water. Dehydration can get ugly." -- Unknown

"On the last day of the feast, the great day, Jesus stood up and cried out, if anyone thirsts, let him come to me and drink." -- John 7:37 / ESV

We were recently looking to upgrade our daily water intake, so we began searching for a 64 oz water jug. While shopping, we noticed that numerous brands sell "Motivational Bottles." Messages on the bottles encourage you to keep drinking throughout the day. These reminders say, *"Remember Your Goal," "No Excuses," or "Drink Up."* These messages are not just hyperbole. See, consuming water is essential for your overall wellness. Think of it this way; water carries nutrients and oxygen to your cells. Drinking water helps flush out bacteria from your bladder, assists digestion, improves sleep, clears up your skin, and prevents constipation. Medical and emotional studies also show that replacing caffeine-loaded drinks with water will lead to weight loss and improved health. Thus, one of the wisest choices you can make toward a wellness lifestyle is drinking water because it hydrates your body. Likewise, your soul needs to be hydrated. Psalm 42:2 says, *"My soul thirsts for God, for the living God. When can I go and meet with God?"* Thirst is ultimately an intense desire. We usually do not think of water as something we crave because we are blessed to live in a country where clean water is readily available. However, we are not looking for coffee, soda, or something sweet when dehydrated. Instead, we naturally desire water because God fashioned our bodies to require it. That is why the Psalmist said "his soul" had a genuine thirst for the Lord. He was saying that his spirit was parched, yet his desire was for nothing else but God. Sometimes we are dried up and need to be replenished, so we go to God. Other times it can just be that we are drinking from the fountain of faith to maintain a spiritual connection with God.

Seeking God will quench your thirst and refuel your soul. Jesus said in John 4:14, *"Whoever drinks of the water that I will give him shall never thirst; but the water that I will give him will become in him a well of water springing up to eternal life."*

Thinking About My Inspiration

Reflective Thinking: *"Your soul needs to be hydrated."*

Review Verse: John 7:37, *"On the last day of the feast, the great day, Jesus stood up and cried out, "If anyone thirsts, let him come to me and drink."*

Responsive Prayer: *"Lord, refresh me with your Word and Spirit."* *Amen*

NOTES

Isolation Is Unhealthy | Day 22

"Solitude is a chosen separation for refining your soul. Isolation is what you crave when you neglect the first." -- Wayne Cordeiro, Pastor, Author

"Whoever isolates himself seeks his own desire; he breaks out against all sound judgment." -- Proverbs 18:1 / ESV

Although it may have different operational names, the strategy of Divide and Conquer is a common tactic in battle. World empires and militaries from other countries are not the only ones who have utilized this method of madness; our enemy, the devil, seeks to cause as much division, confusion, and separation as possible. Perhaps the biggest reason for applying this technique is because isolation is unhealthy. That would explain the legitimate medical concerns for children, teens, and those living alone during the quarantine. So no matter how you slice it, isolation is an unhealthy craving!

See, isolation is dangerous because it leaves you vulnerable and susceptible to satan's lies. You start thinking of unhealthy thoughts, and your anxiety and fears eventually attack your faith. Additionally, seclusion prevents you from reaching your potential and fulfilling the Scripture's numerous "One Another" commands. The divide and conquer strategy can be seen as "clear as day" for church service. The last place that hell wants you is God's house. You will get distracted and even discouraged from being in fellowship at the church. Notice you will not experience that same pressure, whether it's subliminal or not, if you are trying to go to the bar or the club. There will be no demonic resistance if you're looking to get drunk, high, or making some other decision that you will live to regret. However, weather, sleep, and even hairstyles determine our attendance when it comes to church. Also, thoughts that *"I am not good enough," "Nobody likes me there,"* or *"It's okay not to go"* will often fill our heads because isolation is the goal of hell.

Therefore, protect the priority of church attendance in this new year. Make Sundays a day of reverence to the Lord and seek to encourage others to do the same because we are better together!

Hebrews 10:24-25 says, *"And let us consider how we may spur one another on toward love and good deeds, 25 not giving up meeting together, as some are in the habit of doing, but encouraging one another—and all the more as you see the Day approaching."*

Thinking About My Inspiration

Reflective Thinking: *"Isolation is an unhealthy craving."*

Review Verse: Proverbs 18:1, *"Whoever isolates himself seeks his own desire; he breaks out against all sound judgment."*

Responsive Prayer: *Help me Lord not isolate myself from others and your plans. Grant me strength and peace of mind. Amen*

NOTES

Keep Making Prayer A Priority | Day 23

"The key is not to prioritize what's on your schedule, but to schedule your priorities." -- Stephen Covey, Author, Businessman

"Very early in the morning, while it was still dark, Jesus got up, left the house, and went off to a solitary place, where he prayed." –
- Mark 1:35

Early African converts to Christianity were dedicated and consistent in private devotions. Each one reportedly had a spot beyond the bushes where he would pour his heart out to God. Over time the paths to these places became well-worn. As a result, if one of these believers began to neglect prayer, it was soon apparent to the others. They would kindly remind the negligent one, *"Brother, the grass grows on your path."*

Perhaps life's distractions have led to some grass growing on your prayer path. Maybe it's been so long that even weeds are starting to emerge! Regardless of the landscape of your pathway to prayer, you need to seek God now! The key is establishing that prayer will be your top priority. Yes, the responsibilities of a new year or beginning can become taxing on your time. Also, everyday commitments like family, work, or school require you to be all in, but these ethical commitments will only enhance if prayer becomes a daily part of your life. Along those lines, hobbies, socializing, and working out are encouraged but not at the expense of your walk with God.

Thus, Scripture repeatedly teaches us to prioritize prayer with the following directives: In Matthew 6:6a, Jesus said, *"And when you pray..."* Notice that Jesus didn't say "if" you pray or "when you get around to it" the idea is prayer needs to be a regular part of how you communicate with God.

The Old Testament also teaches this practice. Jeremiah 33:3 says, *"Call to me, and I will answer you and will tell you great and hidden things that you have not known."*

Back over in the New Testament, Paul told the church at Thessalonica, *"pray without ceasing"* (First, Thessalonians 5:17). A similar command was given in Colossians 4:2, which says, *"Continue steadfastly in prayer, being watchful in it with thanksgiving."* The Apostle John wrote that prayer includes confession in First John 1:9, *"If we confess our sins, he is faithful and just to forgive us our sins and to cleanse us from all unrighteousness."*

No matter how many times you crisscross the Bible, you will see commands, instructions, examples, models, and people of prayer.

Knowing this, let us check to see if any grass has begun to grow on our path!

Thinking About My Inspiration

Reflective Thinking: *"We are as close to God as we choose to be."*

Review Verse: Mark 1:35, *"Very early in the morning, while it was still dark, Jesus got up, left the house, and went off to a solitary place, where he prayed."*

Responsive Prayer: Oh God, My Father, convict me when I am not being faithful in seeking you. Amen

NOTES

Trust God's Voice | Day 24

"Listen in silence because if your heart is full of other things, you cannot hear the voice of God." -- Mother Theresa

"Behold, I stand at the door and knock. If anyone hears my voice and opens the door, I will come into him and eat with him, and he with me." -- Revelation 3:20 / ESV

An attorney and his associate experienced an ordeal that reminded them exactly why and how you can trust God's voice. While on a small plane flying back to Anchorage in Alaska, the pilot passed out because he feared flying in cloudy weather. The two lawyers quickly began troubleshooting, but since the pilot was not waking up, their only option was to pick up the radio receiver and call out for help.

Thankfully a freighter pilot heading to Tokyo from Anchorage answered and told the men that he would contact the Anchorage flight tower for them.

Within five minutes, someone from emergency services at the building came over the radio to confirm the circumstances. After doing so, the emergency service worker told the two frightened lawyers that they needed to listen to his voice if they wanted to stay alive. He said to the two men, "You can't see me, but I can see you." He warned them that they were about 4 miles from a mountain and they needed to listen to his instructions or they would crash.

Next, the voice over the radio informed them they were approaching some inclement weather, and it would be best if they didn't focus on the storm but instead remained confident in his voice to guide them to Anchorage. They did so, and now came the time to land the plane.

First, the voice told them to look for lights arranged on the runway in the form of a cross. Then, the voice said, use the cross to get home. Amazingly, the two attorneys had a safe landing because they listened to the voice.

Likewise, we can trust God's voice to avoid the potential crashes and stormy conditions of life. Like these two lawyers, we need to obey what we hear and follow the instructions. In John 10:27, Jesus said, *"My sheep hear my voice, and I know them, and they follow me."*

Following Jesus and listening to His voice means having confidence in knowing He still sees us even if we can't see Him. It means that the conditions may be impossible, but if we are willing to trust Him, His voice will see us through our storms and struggles.

For us, the Bible is our control tower. Thus, God speaks primarily through His Word. Therefore, let us spend time every day listening to and trusting the voice of God because with each new year and opportunity comes unexpected obstacles. Trust God's voice to navigate your life.

Thinking About My Inspiration

Reflective Thinking: *"You can trust God to guide you through impossible situations."*

Review Verse: Revelation 3:20 / ESV *"Behold, I stand at the door and knock. If anyone hears my voice and opens the door, I will come into him and eat with him, and he with me."*

Responsive Prayer: Lord, help me to recognize and trust Your voice. Amen

NOTES

Pay Now, Play Later | Day 25

"Time is really the only capital that any human being has and the only thing he cannot afford to lose." -- Thomas Edison, Inventor

"Hard work means prosperity; only a fool idles away his time." -- Proverbs 12:11 / TLB

Success relies on time management. Your ability to wisely handle the twenty-four hours you get each day determines your direction and durability. Often we blame things like burnout or burdens as the reason we do not see breakthroughs, but there's more to the story if we are willing to be transparent. See, if we adopt the time management principle that says, Pay now, play later, we will increase our productivity, fulfill our purpose, and experience the pleasures that God approves.

Think of it this way: Pay now involves health; for example, getting proper sleep, eating healthy, exercising, and steering clear of harmful substances. Doing so leads to a healthier version of yourself and will ultimately make you more effective in the office, classroom, field, job site, or house. Pay now means you put in the work, such as being responsible with your job, school assignments, training, and personal tasks. When we do this, our creditability goes through the roof, and we sharpen our skills simultaneously. More importantly, paying now means you give God the first fruits of your time, talents, and treasures. When we take these accountability steps, we can enjoy life better and humbly wait on God's blessing. Thus, "Play later" represents doing things like sports, entertainment, recreation, vacation, hobbies, or activities after following through on your obligations.

Scripture provides excellent counsel for time management. Psalm 39:4-5 says, *"Lord, remind me how brief my time on earth will be. Remind me that my days are numbered— how fleeting my life is. 5 You have made my life no longer than the width of my hand. My entire lifetime is just a moment to you; at best, each of us is but a breath."*

Ephesians 5:15-17 says, *"Look carefully then how you walk, not as unwise but as wise,16 making the best use of the time because the days are evil.17 Therefore do not be foolish, but understand what the will of the Lord is."* And Colossians 4:5 states, *"Walk in wisdom toward outsiders, making the best use of the time."*

With these verses in mind, a tangible next step is to get into the practice of dedicating your day to the Lord each morning. Ask Him to help you be efficient and proficient in all you do. Next, carefully comb through your current schedule. Check to see what or who needs to be eliminated. Is there anything in the "play category" that is superseding God's plans and your duties?

Remember, you can significantly reduce stress by putting these perspectives into practice.

Thinking About My Inspiration

Reflective Thinking: *"I need to manage my time wisely."*

Review Verse: Proverbs 12:11, *"Hard work means prosperity; only a fool idles away his time."*

Responsive Prayer: Lord, teach me to number my days and be productive what the time that you give to me. Amen

NOTES

Struggling With Negative Self-Talk? | Day 26

"Believing in negative thoughts is the single greatest obstruction to success." — *Charles F. Glassman, Physician*

"Fix your thoughts on what is true and good and right. Think about things that are pure and lovely, and dwell on the fine, good things in others. Think about all you can praise God for and be glad about." -- Philippians 4:8 / TLB

Whether you realize it or not, there is a constant conversation within your mind. You are most likely talking to yourself right now! I recently read a report in which researchers concluded that most people speak at a rate of 150 to 200 words per minute, but they said the internal dialogue that you carry on with yourself (self-talk) is more like 1,300 words per minute.

Thus, the honest question is, how many of those approximately 1,300 words are negative? If your self-talk is negative, the rest of your perspective will suffer, including your interaction with others. Another clear and present dangerous reality of negative self-talk is that you will begin to dwell on defeating and discouraging thoughts.

Therefore, you want to recognize and take proper recourse against negative self-talk.

First, begin by identifying negative self-talk. Contributors to mental health awareness say, *"Negative self-talk is any inner dialogue you have with yourself that may be limiting your ability to believe in yourself and your abilities and reach your potential. It is any thought that diminishes you and your ability to make positive changes in your life or your confidence in your ability to do so."*

After you have put a face to negative self-talk, aim at addressing the problem. Long before there was the Dr. Phil show or psychology books, God said that your thoughts ultimately shape your life.

Proverbs 4:23 says, *"Be careful how you think; your life is shaped by your thoughts."*

Therefore, you must change your thinking if you want to overcome negative self-talk and negativity in your life. Ephesians 4:23 says, *"Let the Spirit change your way of thinking."*

Allowing the Holy Spirit to change your mind includes prayer and the conscious choice to fix your thoughts on what is truthful and right. Philippians 4:8 in The Living Bible says, "Fix your thoughts on what is true and good and right . . . Think about all you can praise God for and be glad about it."

Your mind is the battlefield where negativity fights for control. "Think about all you can praise God for." Then, you will win the war on thoughts and be victorious over negativity.

Thinking About My Inspiration

Reflective Thinking: *"You can win the battle between your ears."*

Review Verse: Philippians 4:8 / TLB, *Fix your thoughts on what is true and good and right. Think about things that are pure and lovely, and dwell on the fine, good things in others. Think about all you can praise God for and be glad about."*

Responsive Prayer: Lord, help me with my mind. Remind me of your truth and lift this discouragement from my thoughts. Amen

NOTES

Slow Start, Strong Finish | Day 27

"It's not where you start — It's where you finish that counts." – Zig Ziglar, Author

"I can do all things through him who strengthens me." -- Philippians 4:13 / ESV

Some people have a slow start in life. It may be a medical issue from birth. It could be poverty-stricken circumstances. There may have been a series of bad breaks and foolish decisions, or maybe it's the result of having had no one in your corner. Whatever the reason, some start slow, but they don't stay there. Consider these well-known contributors and their slow starts:

Winston Churchill seemed so dull as a youth that his father thought he might be incapable of earning a living in England. G.K. Chesterton, the English writer, could not read until he was eight. Then, one of his teachers told him, *"If we could open your head, we should not find any brain but only a lump of white fat."* Thomas Edison's first teacher described him as *"addled,"* while his father almost convinced him he was a *"dunce."*

Albert Einstein's parents feared their child was dull, and he performed so poorly in all high school courses except mathematics that a teacher asked him to drop out.

We even see some notable characters in the Bible experience slow starts to their mission. Moses had a speech impediment and his sister, Miriam, was a gossip. David was considered too small for battle, and Hosea's wife was a prostitute. Jonah ran from God, Elijah was burned out, and Jeremiah was depressed. Gideon and Thomas both doubted God. John Mark was sent home by Paul. Martha was a workaholic, Paul had a past, and the disciples were afraid.

We must remember that God's purposes will prevail because He has the final say. Proverbs 16:1 in the CEV translation says, *"We humans make plans, but the Lord has the final word."*

Knowing this, approach every unfavorable medical report with faith, every difficulty with prayer, every unkind word with resolve in the Lord, and every setback with patience.

Refocus on the fact that it is not how you start but how you finish the race. Second Timothy 4:7, *"I have fought the good fight, I have finished the race, I have kept the faith."*

Thinking About My Inspiration

Reflective Thinking: "You can overcome a slow start in life."

Review Verse: Philippians 4:13 / ESV, *"I can do all things through Christ who strengthens me."*

Responsive Prayer: Lord, no matter what has happened, You have the final say. Help me to trust Your perfect timing and provision. Amen

NOTES

Reevaluate Your Goals | Day 28

"What you get by achieving your goals is not as important as what you become by achieving your goals." — Zig Ziglar

"Make it your goal to live a quiet life, minding your own business and working with your hands, just as we instructed you before." -- First, Thessalonians 4:11

An old business proverb says, *"What gets measured gets managed."* The idea is that examining your position or lack thereof is essential to the overall pursuit of progress. See, at about the four-week mark of any new start, you should take out time to reevaluate your goals.

Ask questions like *"Am I on the right path?" "Anything to improve?" "Have I compromised my values?" "Did I hit the target?" "What do I need to do to meet my objectives?"* These questions and others like them will help you reach your goals.

However, some people may try to persuade you away from being savvy in this area. They say, *"Shouldn't we leave everything to God?"* or *"God will do it, just wait on Him!"*

These examples raise valid points, but we must remember that setting goals are a statement of faith and trust in God. Take the story of the commanding Roman Officer seeking Jesus' help to heal one of his men who was paralyzed. He had a combination of faith and humility, which Jesus noticed and highlighted. Matthew 8:13 says, Jesus said to the Centurion, *"Go; let it be done for you according to your faith. And the servant was healed in that hour."*

Another miracle regarding two blind men who approached Jesus for mercy ends with a similar result. Matthew 9:29, *"Then he touched their eyes, saying, "According to your faith be it done to you."* In both situations, the word faith can symbolize a goal. It was the Centurion Officals' goal for his soldier to walk. Similarly, it was the goal of the blind men to find mercy. You can do the same; take a righteous request, such as helping others or asking God to be merciful and make it a goal. Perhaps you are praying for a new job, a move, a health need, financial provision, or a spiritual transformation. Make the pursuit a goal to reach and pray about it daily.

Another factor about the Centurion and the two blind men is their faith required action. You will notice that faith and goals often depend on discipline and diligence. When you do so, the blessing of success isn't far behind. Proverbs 21:5 says, *"Good planning and hard work lead to prosperity, but hasty shortcuts lead to poverty."*

Knowing this, set financial, professional, personal, emotional, physical, and relational goals. While all those goals are merit-worthy, the best ones you can put in place are spiritual ones.

Philippians 3:14, *"I press on toward the goal for the prize of the upward call of God in Christ Jesus."*

May God bless you as you pursue the goals that God gives to you.

Thinking About My Inspiration

Reflective Thinking: *"What gets measured gets managed."*

Review Verse: First, Thessalonians 4:11 / NIV, *"Make it your goal* *to live a quiet life, minding your own business and working with your hands, just as we instructed you before."*

Responsive Prayer: My Father and my God direct my goals and steps. Let all that I do honor you. Amen

NOTES

Defeating Discouragement | Day 29

"Discouragement can be temporary-or it can destroy our life. The choice is ours. If we refuse to deal with discouragement head-on, we are opening the door for it to completely dominate our life." -- Charles Stanley, Pastor, Author

"The Lord himself goes before you and will be with you; he will never leave you nor forsake you. Do not be afraid; do not be discouraged." -- Deuteronomy 31:8 / NIV

Like an aggressive disease, discouragement poses a threat to your overall health. However, you can conquer this condition because discouragement is curable.

To defeat discouragement, you need to know the causes and the cures.

But, first, recognize that fear leads to discouragement. Whenever you are afraid, your adversity seems a lot bigger, and there appears to be no light at the end of the tunnel.

Secondly, failure can produce discouragement. Suffering a setback and not hitting your goals will put you in the tank, emotionally and relationally speaking. As a result, you isolate yourself or become indecisive because discouragement has replaced determination.

Thirdly, fatigue can contribute to discouragement. Working hard has a price. The reality is that burning the candle on both ends will render you tired and vulnerable to discouraging thoughts.

Fourth, frustration will undoubtedly produce discouragement. Life can be unpredictable and sometimes downright unfair. In these moments, frustration will consume you, quickly becoming an "overwhelming despair" that is tough to handle.

Finally, fake behavior of any kind invites discouragement. The notion, "Fake it till you make it," is a foolish focus because after you come off the high of pretending, you plummet like a stock that has lost value. Look no further than social media. People make these gushing posts about their lives. Meanwhile, they are unhappy and have one foot out the door. We must remember that facades always end in discouragement because reality eventually sets in, and our mental health sinks like a brick thrown into the ocean.

Thus, to cure and overcome discouragement, you need to focus your thoughts on God's promises. Isaiah 41:10 says, *"Don't be afraid, for I am with you. Don't be discouraged, for I am your God. I will strengthen you and help you. I will hold you up with my victorious right hand."*

Next, you need the right friends in your corner. Second Corinthians 7:6 says, *"God, who encourages those who are discouraged, encouraged us by the arrival of Titus."* *You must have people in your life who will refresh you and be willing to tell you what you need to hear, not what you want to hear.*

By God's grace, you will survive and thrive past your discouragement. Psalm 42:5 *"Why am I discouraged? Why is my heart so sad? I will put my hope in God! I will praise him again—my Savior and my God!"*

Thinking About My Inspiration

Reflective thinking: "Discouragement can be temporary- or it can destroy our life."

Review Verse: Deuteronomy 31:8 / NIV, *"The Lord himself goes before you and will be with you; he will never leave you nor forsake you. Do not be afraid; do not be discouraged."*

Responsive Prayer: Lord, Help me get through my trials of discouragement. Amen

NOTES

"I can't imagine a person becoming a success who doesn't give this game of life everything he's got." – Walter Cronkite, New Anchorman

"A hard worker has plenty of food, but a person who chases fantasies has no sense." -- Proverbs 12:11 / NLT

History tells the story of many bizarre and boneheaded pursuits. One of them was by a farmer back in 1847 named George Donner and others from Springfield, Illinois. These rural ranchers and fellow citizens were spellbound over tales of incredible riches in California. Thus, they set out on a dangerous trip to find their treasure. One of the men responsible for leading the expedition was James Reed, who claimed to have a special route to save time.

However, his map was based on rumors, and like his smooth-talking promises about riches, he was dead wrong. Sadly, many in the group traveling by wagons through the mountains and badlands died from freezing temperatures. In the big picture, these people were blinded by their desire to be rich, and the pursuit proved to be a failure and produced a fatal ending. We may not have gold fever or thoughts of acquiring free land, but we have pursued our share of dead ends. Thankfully, the Scriptures teach us to chase what matters. Proverbs 21:21 says, *"Whoever pursues righteousness and unfailing love will find life, righteousness, and honor."*

We must remember that God will always bless those seeking His purposes and approved pathways. However, we must also not forget that this perspective doesn't guarantee smooth sailing. There will be some setbacks and storms along the way, but God is faithful, and He will see you through because where He guides, He provides.

On the contrary, when we believe and follow the lie of a faster and easier way of blessing that God does not endorse, we should expect delays and disappointments at best. Orrin Woodward said, *"You will find that there are many shortcuts that lead to failure, but there are no shortcuts to true success."*

See, chasing what matters in life is what our heavenly Father wants for His children. As Third John 1:4 says, *"I have no greater joy than this: to hear that my children are walking in truth."*

Let us focus on chasing what matters!

Thinking About My Inspiration

Reflective Thinking: *"God will always bless the person seeking after His purposes and approved pathways."*

Review Verse: Proverbs 12:11 / NLT, *"A hard worker has plenty of food, but a person who chases fantasies has no sense."*

Responsive Prayer: Lord, direct my focus to chase what you approve. Amen

NOTES

Get In Agreement With God | Day 31

"God doesn't work on our timetable. He has a plan that He will execute perfectly and for the highest, greatest good of all, and for His ultimate glory." — Dr. Charles R. Swindoll, Professor

"Seek first his kingdom and his righteousness, and all these things will be given to you as well." -- Matthew 6:33 / NIV

Walking with someone for a considerable distance requires being on the same page with that person. That means you keep a similar pace, maintain good communication, and perhaps share the same destination.

Likewise, your relationship with God often referred to as *"a walk,"* operates similarly. Amos 3:3 says, *"Can two walk together, except they be agreed?"* See, the key to having a healthy walk with God is to agree with Him and His Word. While this sounds nice, what exactly does it mean? First, you need to follow God's commands, such as confession, consistency, commitment, and church. That means we shouldn't treat what God says in His Word as a recommendation or a suggestion. Agreement with God comes with obedience first. Secondly, you need to connect to the Lord through prayer. Daily communication through prayer and fasting is essential to growing your walk. Thirdly, you need to share God's destination for your life. Knowing your purpose and serving God is vital in agreeing with Him.

Several notable characters and passages in the Scriptures provide examples of this type of walk with God. Genesis 5:24 says, *"Enoch walked with God; then he was not there because God took him."* Genesis 6:9 says, *"These are the family records of Noah. Noah was a righteous man, blameless among his contemporaries; Noah walked with God."* Although Job's friends gave their unsolicited advice, which wasn't necessarily applicable to him, the general counsel is correct. Job 22:21, *"Agree with God, and be at peace; thereby good will come to you."* In Galatians 5:16, Paul told the church at Galatia to consider their walk, *"I say, then, walk by the Spirit, and you will certainly not carry out the desire of the flesh."*

Comparing these verses provides the counsel that says, *"To walk with God, you need to be in agreement with Him."*

By God's grace, your walk with Him will be strong and steady. First John 2:6 tells us, *"The one who says he abides in Him ought himself to walk in the same manner as He walked."*

Thinking About My Inspiration

Reflective Thinking: "God will always bless the person seeking after His purposes and approved pathways."

Review Verse: Matthew 6:33 / NIV, *"Seek first his kingdom and his righteousness, and all these things will be given to you as well."*

Responsive Prayer: Lord, I want to walk in agreement with you. Convict me of any wrong direction that I am following. Amen

NOTES

Your Greatest Inspiration | Day 32

"The best and most beautiful things in the world cannot be seen or even touched - they must be felt with the heart." — Helen Keller.

"Jesus answered, 'I am the way and the truth and the life. No one comes to the Father except through me.' -- John 14:6 / NIV

You will find some very encouraging stories as you survey and scroll social media feeds. For example, I have read about children overcoming disease, weight loss testimonies, people rising above addiction, reconciliation for relationships, and accomplishments that defied the odds. All wonderful and uplifting! In addition, certain movies, sporting events, music, and books convey hope to help change and, at times, challenge your perspective for the better. However, as incredible as those are, they have a short shelf life in terms of providing ongoing motivation and perseverance. That's not to take away from those accounts; instead, it explains that we need a lasting and legitimate inspiration, and that source is Jesus Christ.

With humble yet unmatched strength, Christ willingly went to the cross to endure the punishment of sin even though He was sinless!

Philippians 2:8 says, *"...He humbled himself in obedience to God and died a criminal's death on a cross."* He accepted this mission to provide everlasting mercy and atonement for our sins. By choosing God's gift of salvation which includes the forgiveness of sins and eternal life, you become a follower of Christ. Whether we realize it or not, everyone needs repentance and faith in Jesus. Romans 3:23 states, *"for everyone has sinned; we all fall short of God's glorious standard."* Romans 6:23 says, *"For the wages of sin is death, but the free gift of God is eternal life through Christ Jesus our Lord."*

God has graciously given us His Son, and upon acceptance of Him, we will be saved from sin and never have to fear eternal separation from the Lord. Romans 10:9 tells us, *"If you openly declare that Jesus is Lord and believe in your heart that God raised him from the dead, you will be saved."*

Your secure position in Christ will lead to an enduring and genuine inspiration that will not fade away. As you grow in your faith, you will see that life in Christ will guide you toward an extraordinary life. Jesus said in John 10:10, *"...I came so that they would have life, and have it abundantly."*

Faith in Jesus Christ means that you have peace with God and that you get to enjoy the peace of God. It also helps you to discover His plan through the Scriptures and develop a sense of purpose. Over time, you begin to desire a holy type of pleasure. You are drawn to participate in work greater than yourself. These feelings result from God's blessings and inspiration through His Son, Jesus.

If you haven't done so, open your heart to God and ask Christ into your life. Receive His forgiveness, promise of eternal life, and inspiration that will carry you through even the darkest days. You can do this by repeating this simple prayer:

Dear Lord, *I am a sinner who lacks peace in my soul. I believe in your Son, Jesus Christ. I believe that He died for my sins and rose from the dead. I repent of my ways and ask Him to be my savior and Lord. Grant me forgiveness and eternal life, and be my inspiration every day. Amen.*

Congratulations on praying this special prayer! It will be necessary now to grow in your faith. You start immediately by reading through the Gospel of John each day.

For those who have already placed their faith in Christ, allow this devotional book to guide you into a more profound, consistent commitment to your faith. There's no telling how far you can soar when Christ is your inspiration!

Thinking About My Inspiration

Reflective Thinking: "Jesus is our greatest source of inspiration."

Review Verse: John 14:6 / NIV, *"Jesus answered, "I am the way and the truth and the life. No one comes to the Father except through me."*

Responsive Prayer: Thank you, God, for your Son Jesus and the inspiration He gives me to pursue your plans. Amen

NOTES

Congratulations are completing this devotional book. I pray you were encouraged and challenged to make healthy choices. Over time, these good decisions will help strengthen your faith and focus! Please share any feedback and testimony with me by sending an email to ray@crossroadsny.org

Stay tuned for more devotional-style books to come!

Made in the USA
Coppell, TX
19 December 2022

90197567R00085